W9-BOS-002

JAN   2020

WORK IN THE
MILITARY

by Roberta Baxter

BrightP◆int Press

San Diego, CA

BrightPoint Press

3 1969 02673 2676

© 2020 BrightPoint Press
an imprint of ReferencePoint Press, Inc.
Printed in the United States

For more information, contact:
BrightPoint Press
PO Box 27779
San Diego, CA 92198
www.BrightPointPress.com

LIBRARY OF CONGRESS CATALOGING-IN-PUBLICATION DATA

Names: Baxter, Roberta, 1952- author.
Title: Work in the military / Roberta Baxter.
Description: San Diego, CA : ReferencePoint Press, Inc., [2020] | Series: Career finder | Includes index. | Audience: Grades 9-12.
Identifiers: LCCN 2019005398 (print) | LCCN 2019005505 (ebook) | ISBN 9781682827307 (ebook) | ISBN 9781682827291 (hardcover)
Subjects: LCSH: United States--Armed Forces--Vocational guidance.
Classification: LCC UB147 (ebook) | LCC UB147 .B36 2020 (print) | DDC 355.0023/73--dc23
LC record available at https://lccn.loc.gov/2019005398

CONTENTS

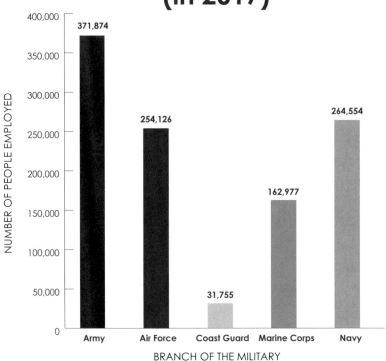

Employment in the Military (in 2017)

Military Personnel (in 2017)

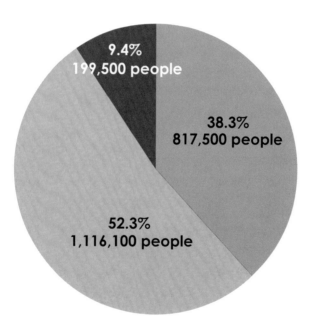

9.4%
199,500 people

38.3%
817,500 people

52.3%
1,116,100 people

- Reserve and National Guard
- Deployed in United States
- Deployed Overseas

WHAT IS THE MILITARY?

A group of people marches along a road. The marchers wear military uniforms. They carry heavy bags on their backs. The bags are full of gear. The gear includes ammunition and first aid kits. The marchers also carry rifles. They are in Basic Combat Training (BCT). They are preparing for a job in the US Army. BCT is ten

Many military positions include physical training in addition to other more specialized skills.

weeks long. Those who pass the training

will become soldiers.

People who work in the US military

have important jobs. They protect and

Members of the military work together to make sure they are ready to enter combat at a moment's notice.

defend the United States. The military has five branches. The US Army mainly fights enemies on the ground. The US Air Force often fights from the air. The US Navy mainly fights at sea. The US Marine Corps is a special force. Marines respond to emergencies. They protect Army bases.

The US Coast Guard patrols US waters. It often searches for and rescues people.

Each military branch has ranks, or levels. The ranks are grouped into two major categories: **enlisted** members and officers. Enlisted people follow commands and complete tasks. Enlisted people make up about 82 percent of the military. New members of the military are called privates or recruits. They are the lowest rank. People move up in rank by gaining experience and passing tests.

Officers lead enlisted people. They also have ranks. The lowest rank is lieutenant or ensign. The highest is general or admiral. Officers can move up in rank by taking on more responsibilities.

Work in the military is different from other jobs. People who enlist in the military cannot just quit. They have promised to serve for at least three to six years. The length of service depends on which military jobs they choose. They can serve longer than that.

Many people in the military are away from their families for long periods of time. They might be **deployed** overseas. Members of the US military serve around the world.

Drill sergeants oversee the training of new Army recruits.

Most move to a new place every three or four years. They go wherever the military needs them. Military jobs are difficult. But they can also be rewarding. Military service members are proud to defend their country.

CHAPTER ONE

MARINE CORPS RIFLEMAN

Marines are often the first to fight in any conflict. Marines can have specializations. Some are pilots. Others are trained for ground combat. Marine Corps riflemen have special skills. They are experts in using rifles and other weapons. They support other marines in ground combat.

JOB CODE: Military occupational specialty (MOS) 0311

MINIMUM EDUCATION: High school diploma or General Educational Diploma

PERSONAL QUALITIES: Between seventeen and twenty-nine years old, a US citizen or permanent resident, in top physical and mental condition

WORKING CONDITIONS: Marine Corps riflemen are deployed around the world.

TRAINING: Boot camp and Marine Rifleman Course at the School of Infantry

MILITARY RANK: Enlisted, private through sergeant

SALARY: About $19,660 to $39,700 per year, depending on rank and the number of years served

NUMBER OF JOBS: In 2017, 40,108 people were employed as Marine Corps combat personnel.

WHAT THEY DO

Many people start out as riflemen in the

Marines. Marine Corps rifleman is an

Marine Corps riflemen are trained to use many different types of weapons.

entry-level position. People usually move on to higher-level positions in the Marines after gaining experience as riflemen.

Riflemen are organized into fire teams. Each team has three people. Each person has a rifle. One person is the leader.

Fire teams are grouped into squads.

A squad is made up of three fire teams.

The squad has a leader and an assistant

leader. Each squad also has a systems

operator. This person uses communications

equipment. The squads work independently

or together in larger groups. Officers are in

charge of groups larger than squads.

Riflemen have different jobs within

each squad. In some squads, they are the

leaders. They may go behind enemy lines.

They gather important information about

the enemy. This information includes an

enemy force's size, strength, and location.

The riflemen report this information back to marine commanders. In other squads, riflemen are in charge of the weapons. Riflemen can also be rifle platoon guides. A platoon is a group made up of three or four squads. Rifle platoon guides make sure everyone in the platoon is fed. They also make sure everyone has enough ammunition.

All marines have special gear. They wear helmets to protect their heads. They wear body armor. They carry heavy packs with supplies. The supplies include a radio, canteen, and ammunition. **GPS** units and

Riflemen work together to accomplish their missions.

compasses help them track their location.

They carry rifles and other weapons.

TRAINING

A high school diploma is usually needed to

qualify for the Marine Corps. People who

Marines have to practice putting on and carrying all of their gear.

want to enlist in the military can take the

Armed Services Vocational Aptitude Battery

(ASVAB) test. The US Department of

Defense (DoD) developed this test. The test

determines which military jobs would be the best fit for a person. High school students who are interested in the military can take this test. It helps them decide which military career to pursue.

All Marine Corps recruits must go through boot camp. This is a training period. It lasts twelve weeks. There are two locations for this training. Women go to Parris Island in South Carolina. The other location is San Diego, California. Men can train at either location.

Each week of boot camp is full of hard physical training. The training includes runs, sit-ups, and pull-ups. Recruits also learn special skills. They learn how to use rifles and other weapons. They learn how to clean, take apart, and put together rifles. They practice working together as teams. They must pass a swimming test and first aid training.

Recruits must graduate from boot camp to become marines. Then they move on to the School of **Infantry** (SOI). There are two school locations. Recruits who graduate from San Diego go to SOI West. SOI West is in Pendleton, California. Those who graduate from Parris Island go to SOI East.

Marine Corps recruits learn many skills, such as hand-to-hand combat, in boot camp.

SOI East is in Jacksonville, North Carolina.

At these schools, marines work in training

battalions. A battalion is a group of military

troops. Marines who want to specialize

Some marines also train at the Mountain Warfare Training Center in Bridgeport, California. They practice hiking through mountains and difficult terrain.

train with Infantry Training Battalions.

They go through fifty-nine days of training.

Those who want to become riflemen take

the Marine Rifleman Course. They learn

advanced skills in shooting different weapons, such as **mortars**.

After completing this training, marines are assigned to a base. They meet other marines in their fire team and squad. They train daily. Training is an important part of a marine's job. Marines must be able to run and hike long distances while carrying a heavy pack.

Marine Corps training is physically and mentally difficult. Marines work long days. A marine can be deployed at any time. Marines are stationed around the world.

Some bases are in the United States. Others are in other countries.

LOOKING AHEAD

Marines provide an important service. They help defend the country. They are always needed. First Lieutenant Marina A. Hierl is a marine. She leads a platoon of thirty-five men. She is the first woman to lead an infantry platoon. The *New York Times* interviewed her in 2018. She said, "I wanted to do something important with my life." Marine Corps service is challenging. But marines take pride in serving their country.

FIND OUT MORE

School of Infantry

website: www.whatsafterboot.com/soi.asp

This website explains the next steps for marine training after boot camp.

Today's Military

website: www.todaysmilitary.com/about-military/service-branches/marine-corps

This website gives information about what it is like to serve in the Marines. It talks about how to join and what benefits members receive. It also explores different careers in the Marines.

The US Marine Corps

website: www.marines.com

The official website of the US Marine Corps answers questions about joining the Marines. People can reach out to marines through this website.

CHAPTER TWO

FIELD ARTILLERY OFFICER

The US Army has defended the United States since the country's beginning. This branch of the military fights with infantry. It uses tanks and **artillery**. Artillery weapons are used to fire missiles.

WHAT THEY DO

Field artillery officers work for the US Army. They make plans and use artillery.

JOB CODE: Area of Concentration (AOC) 13A

MINIMUM EDUCATION: A four-year college degree or specialized officer training after serving in the military

PERSONAL QUALITIES: A US citizen or permanent resident, a good leader, skilled in math and science, in top physical and mental condition

WORKING CONDITIONS: Field artillery officers work full time. They may be deployed overseas.

TRAINING: Must complete the Basic Officer Leader Course (BOLC)

MILITARY RANK: Officer, lieutenant through colonel

SALARY: About $37,000 to $123,500 per year, depending on rank and the number of years served

NUMBER OF JOBS: In 2017, 101,873 people were employed as combat personnel in the US Army.

They command groups of enlisted soldiers. These groups are called field artillery units. Each unit is made up of 60 to 200 soldiers. Soldiers and officers transport

Field artillery officers work with many types of heavy weapons.

the artillery. The artillery can include large

cannons, rockets, and missile launchers.

The weapons are on wheels or trucks.

This allows soldiers and officers to move

them around.

Different weapons are needed for different types of combat. Artillery allows soldiers to fight from a distance. These weapons are large. They are dangerous. Missiles travel at high speeds. Officers need training to safely use artillery.

Artillery weapons are powerful. For example, one type of missile is called surface-to-surface. It is launched from the ground or from a ship at sea. It is aimed at a target on the ground. Launch systems can fire these missiles great distances. The Army works to improve launch systems. Then it could launch missiles from even greater distances. In 2018, the Army wanted to double the range of its surface-to-surface missiles. Then the missiles could hit targets 1,400 miles (2,253 km) away. Artillery officers need to know how to use the latest weapons.

TRAINING

There is more than one way to become an Army officer. Some people graduate from the US Military Academy at West Point. This is a military school in West Point, New York. Others join the Reserve Officer Training Corps (ROTC) at a military or nonmilitary college. People who already have college

A small team of people is needed to fire artillery.

degrees can attend the US Army's Officer

Candidate School (OCS). This school is at

Fort Benning in Georgia. Enlisted members

of the military can also attend OCS.

Training to become a field artillery

officer starts with the Basic Officer Leader

West Point is one of the oldest military academies in the world.

Course (BOLC). The course teaches people to lead others. There are two phases of this course: BOLC A and BOLC B. BOLC A is offered through OCS, the ROTC, or the US Military Academy at West Point.

It teaches the basic skills needed to become an officer. BOLC B gives people specialized training. It teaches people about the equipment they will need to use. The BOLC B phase happens at Fort Sill. This is an Army post near Lawton, Oklahoma. About 9,000 officers are trained here each year. They attend the US Army Field Artillery School. They learn how to use artillery. They also learn military tactics and strategies. This training takes eighteen and a half weeks to complete.

John Bushman is a field artillery officer. He attended the Virginia Military Institute.

He went through the ROTC program. He teaches enlisted people basic skills. He shows them how to use and maintain artillery equipment. He said, "Everybody comes to the Army . . . as an individual. And everybody has their own motivations for joining."

LOOKING AHEAD

Field artillery officers spend a lot of time on the firing range. They must practice using artillery often. Lieutenant Emily Bessler is a field artillery officer. She worked hard to become a platoon leader. She trained through the ROTC program. She leads a

The US Army Field Artillery Museum at Fort Sill in Oklahoma shows how US Army artillery has improved over the years.

platoon of about forty soldiers. She may

be deployed on short notice. She can be

deployed anywhere in the world. Bessler

and her platoon train constantly. She said,

Field artillery officers spend many hours on firing ranges. They have to practice staying calm under pressure.

"It's very fast-paced . . . but [it] is incredibly rewarding work." Field artillery officers help protect the country. Field artillery is a major part of the Army's strength. The Army will always need officers to lead in this area.

FIND OUT MORE

Today's Military

website: www.todaysmilitary.com/working/
careers/artillery-and-missile-officers

This website has information about artillery
and missile officer careers.

The US Army: Field Artillery Officer (13A)

website: www.goarmy.com/careers-and-jobs/
browse-career-and-job-categories/combat/
field-artillery-officer.html

The official US Army website has an overview
of the job of field artillery officer. It also shows
similar Army jobs.

The US Army Field Artillery School

website: https://sill-www.army.mil/USAFAS/
who-we-are.html

This website has facts about the US Army
Field Artillery School at Fort Sill. It shares the
school's mission and history. It also gives an
overview of the training process.

CHAPTER THREE

NAVY PILOT

The US Navy serves around the world. Navy ships sail through all the oceans. They dock at ports on every continent. The Navy has a variety of ships. They include cruisers, amphibious assault ships, and destroyers. These ships are designed to fight enemies at sea. They are fast and powerful. The largest ship of all is the aircraft carrier. An aircraft carrier is a large

JOB CODE: **Navy Officer Billet Classification (NOBC) 8501**

MINIMUM EDUCATION: **College degree and completion of Officer Candidate School, followed by a course at Naval Aviation Schools Command**

PERSONAL QUALITIES: **A US citizen or permanent resident, in good physical and mental condition, excellent eyesight, good reflexes**

WORKING CONDITIONS: **Navy pilots are deployed around the world.**

TRAINING: **Flight training**

MILITARY RANK: **Officer, ensign through admiral**

SALARY: **About $37,000 to $189,600 per year, depending on rank and the number of years served**

NUMBER OF JOBS: **In 2017, 6,152 people were employed as officers in the US Navy.**

warship. It has a long, flat deck. Navy

pilots fly and land aircraft on this deck.

Aircraft carriers can transport aircraft all

Navy pilots must learn how to take off from and land on aircraft carrier decks.

over the world. Pilots fly aircraft to carry

out missions.

WHAT THEY DO

Navy pilots are also called aviators. They

protect the aircraft carrier and other ships

on their missions. They pilot high-tech aircraft. They fly **surveillance** missions. Surveillance involves spying on enemies. Navy pilots sometimes fight with enemy planes. They may also carry out rescue missions. They can find and track enemy submarines.

Aircraft are designed for different purposes. Navy pilots' jobs depend on the types of planes they fly. For example, the F/A-18 Hornet is a fighter plane. It attacks an enemy's fighter planes or drops bombs. The P3-Orion detects submarines. It carries weapons such as bombs and **torpedoes**.

These weapons can be used to attack submarines.

TRAINING

All Navy pilots are officers. They must have a college education. Some go to the US Naval Academy in Annapolis, Maryland. Others start in the Naval Reserve Officers Training Corps (NROTC) at other colleges. After college, they attend the US Navy's OCS. This school is in Newport, Rhode Island. The OCS program is twelve weeks long. It teaches important skills. Students learn how to lead and give commands. They also learn how to deal with stress.

Navy planes such as the F/A-18 Hornet are designed to be lightweight and easy to maneuver.

People who want to become Navy pilots must pass the Aviation Selection Test Battery (ASTB). The ASTB tests aviation knowledge. It also tests people's abilities, including their math and reading skills. If they have not had any flight

US Naval Academy graduates throw their hats to celebrate their graduation. Students become officers after they graduate from the academy.

training, they go to a flight school. They

take twenty-five hours of classes. Then

they are ready for preflight training.

They take six weeks of classes at Naval

Aviation Schools Command. This school

is in Pensacola, Florida. They study

topics related to aviation. The topics

include engineering, air navigation, and

water survival.

After preflight training, pilots start primary

flight training. This training takes about

twenty-two weeks. They practice flying and

take more classes. Then they train to use

a specific type of aircraft. They fly more

than one hundred hours in the aircraft.

This allows them to get used to the aircraft.

They become a Navy pilot when they

complete flight training. They each receive a

gold pin in the shape of wings. These pins

show that they are Navy pilots. People call these pins "wings of gold."

Pilots can be deployed anywhere around the world. Some work on aircraft carriers. Others work at naval air stations. These are military bases on land.

LOOKING AHEAD

It takes a lot of time and hard work to become a Navy pilot. The job can be dangerous. Pilots travel to many places around the world. Long separations from family can be hard. But the job can be exciting. Navy pilots may develop lifelong

Learning how to fly complex military aircraft requires a lot of time and training.

friendships. They form strong bonds as they

work together to defend the country.

The US Navy always needs pilots. As

each class of pilots retires or moves on to

The US Navy's famous Blue Angels team is known for its daring aerial stunts.

other jobs, new pilots are needed to take their place.

James Waddell is a Navy pilot. He flies a P-3 Orion plane. He is the third generation in his family to fly for the US Navy. He said, "The beauty of naval aviation is that you never know where on the map it is going to take you."

FIND OUT MORE

Naval Air Station Kingsville

website: www.cnic.navy.mil/regions/cnrse/
installations/nas_kingsville/about/tenant_
commands/training_air_wing_two.html

Pilot training happens at this naval air station. The website has information about how flight training works and what student pilots must learn.

Naval Reserve Officers Training Corps (NROTC)

website: www.nrotc.navy.mil/aviator.html

This website has information about the NROTC and the training that is needed to become a Navy pilot.

The US Navy

website: www.navy.com/careers/naval-aviator

The US Navy website describes the skills and training needed to become a Navy pilot. It also explores the benefits of the job.

CHAPTER FOUR

COAST GUARD ELECTRONICS TECHNICIAN

The US Coast Guard has several missions. It protects US coasts and waterways. It keeps drugs from entering the country. It also rescues people at sea. The Coast Guard uses special equipment to perform these missions. For example, Coast Guard ships have **radar** systems.

JOB CODE: Coast Guard rating ET

MINIMUM EDUCATION: High school diploma or General Educational Diploma

PERSONAL QUALITIES: A US citizen or permanent resident, seventeen to twenty-seven years old, detail-oriented, good at math

WORKING CONDITIONS: Coast Guard electronics technicians can be stationed anywhere along the US coast. Some live on ships called cutters.

TRAINING: Training at Coast Guard electronics technician schools

MILITARY RANK: Enlisted, recruit through master chief petty officer

SALARY: About $19,660 to $72,800, depending on rank and the number of years served

NUMBER OF JOBS: In 2017, 4,351 people worked in electronic and electrical equipment repair for the US Coast Guard.

Radar is used to find objects such as ships.

Electronics technicians (ETs) make sure

Coast Guard equipment runs smoothly.

Electronics technicians repair a light on a Coast Guard ship. Lights help Coast Guard ships navigate in the dark and find other ships.

WHAT THEY DO

The Coast Guard patrols US waters in boats or cutters. Cutters are larger than boats. They are at least 65 feet (19.8 m) long. Crews live onboard cutters.

Many people know the Coast Guard as the search-and-rescue service. That is one of its missions. Coast Guard boats and cutters rescue people. The Coast Guard also uses helicopters. ETs make sure these vehicles can navigate. They operate GPS receivers. GPS helps with navigation. ETs also make sure vehicles can communicate with each other. They install and maintain equipment. This includes communications equipment.

Another Coast Guard mission is homeland security. This involves keeping **terrorists** out of the country. The Coast

Guard has law enforcement teams. These teams patrol coastal waters. They make sure no terrorists enter US waters.

The Coast Guard also keeps the country's ports safe. It makes sure **buoys** and lighthouses are working. These systems help boaters find their way. ETs help with all of these missions.

TRAINING

Coast Guard recruits go through boot camp. This happens at the US Coast Guard Training Center. This center is in Cape May, New Jersey. The training is tough. Trainees run, swim, and tread water.

Some Coast Guard cutters can break through ice. This helps create a path for supply ships in winter.

They do sit-ups and push-ups. They learn

how to use weapons and work as a team.

They also study the history of the Coast

Guard. Boot camp lasts eight weeks.

Coast Guard recruits line up outside the Coast Guard Training Center in Cape May.

Boot camp graduates are called seamen.

They may go on to advanced training.

Electronics technician training is one type of

advanced training.

Training to become an ET comes after

boot camp. Electronics Technician "A"

School teaches people how electronics work. Students learn to read diagrams of electronic equipment. Next, students go to Electronics Technician "C" School. It gives advanced training for a specific electronic system.

Jennifer Foley is an ET for the Coast Guard. She works on a cutter that is based in Virginia. The cutter sails as far as South America. The main job of the workers on the cutter is to intercept illegal drugs. Workers also try to keep people from illegally entering the United States. They perform search-and-rescue operations too.

Foley stands watch in the combat information center. This is the command and control center. Foley monitors the radar system. She makes sure it is working. Radar detects ships or boats that might be carrying illegal drugs.

In 2010, an earthquake hit Haiti. Foley's cutter was the first US military unit that arrived to help. She let the Haitian people know help was coming. She was proud to have been involved in this mission. She said, "I'm not one of the people who goes out on the small boat and actually does the lifesaving. . . . But I'm still part of an

A cutter's combat information center contains radios and communications equipment.

organization that goes out and that makes

a difference."

LOOKING AHEAD

The Coast Guard relies on electronic

systems. The Coast Guard regularly

The Coast Guard relies on many types of equipment to perform search-and-rescue missions. Electronics technicians maintain some of this equipment.

updates its equipment. There is always a

need for people to operate and maintain

this equipment. ETs are in high demand.

FIND OUT MORE

Forcecom: Force Readiness Command

website: www.forcecom.uscg.mil/Our-Organization/FORCECOM-UNITS/TraCen-Petaluma/Training/ET

Learn about what happens at Electronics Technician "A" and "C" schools at this website.

Today's Military

website: www.todaysmilitary.com/careers-benefits/career-stories/jennifer-foley

Read an interview with a Coast Guard ET at this site.

The US Coast Guard

website: www.gocoastguard.com/active-duty-careers/enlisted-opportunities/view-job-descriptions/et

This website describes the training needed to become an ET. It also explores what the job involves.

CHAPTER FIVE

AIR FORCE CYBER SYSTEMS OPERATIONS SPECIALIST

The US Air Force flies planes. It also launches and tracks satellites. Satellites are machines that orbit Earth. Some satellites are part of a navigation system. This system is called GPS. GPS satellites send radio signals to receivers on Earth.

JOB CODE: **Air Force Specialty Code (AFSC) 3D0X2**

MINIMUM EDUCATION: **High school diploma or General Educational Diploma**

PERSONAL QUALITIES: **Between seventeen and thirty-nine years old, a US citizen or permanent resident, good with computers, a good communicator**

WORKING CONDITIONS: **Cyber specialists can work on any US Air Force base.**

TRAINING: **Basic training and tech school**

MILITARY RANK: **Enlisted, recruit through master sergeant**

SALARY: **About $19,660 to $72,800, depending on rank and the number of years served**

NUMBER OF JOBS: **In 2017, 50,708 people worked as engineering, science, and technical personnel for the US Air Force.**

For example, a cell phone is a type of GPS receiver. It calculates its distance from the satellites. This helps people figure out where they are. It helps them with directions.

The DoD developed the GPS satellite network in the 1970s. GPS helped with military navigation. Today many people rely on GPS. The Air Force maintains the satellites in space.

The Air Force also has cyber operations. The word *cyber* comes from *cyberspace*. Cyberspace refers to computer networks and the internet. Cyber Systems Operations specialists protect computer networks. Their field of work is called cybersecurity.

WHAT THEY DO

Computer networks connect people. But they are vulnerable. People may try to

Cyber Systems Operations specialists help protect military computers from cyberattacks.

break into networks. They try to shut down

networks. Or they try to steal information.

Some networks store important information.

The military's network has information about

the US military. This can include information

about weapons or military plans. It is

important to protect these military secrets.

Cyber specialists design computer networks. They also install networks. They provide tech support. They monitor attacks on the networks. Their goal is to stop these attacks. They keep up-to-date on new cybersecurity threats.

Cyber specialists are part of the Air Force Reserve. There are about 68,000 people in the Air Force Reserve. They make up 20 percent of the Air Force. Reserve members are trained fighting units. They can be called to combat if the Air Force needs them. They may be needed in times of war. Or they may be needed during a

Military planes rely on computers to get to their destinations and complete their missions.

national emergency. They are backup for

active-duty units. Active-duty units are

people who serve overseas.

The reserve offers many types of

careers. Cyber specialist is just one job

among many. Other people are health care

professionals. They give health care

The Air Force also uses computers for surveillance missions.

to military personnel. Still others help

plan military missions. There are many

opportunities in the reserve. Reserve

personnel provide important services.

TRAINING

Some people enter the Air Force Reserve

after serving in the military. But military

service is not required to apply for the reserve. Cyber specialists are enlisted personnel. People who enlist in the Air Force first attend basic training. They learn about the Air Force's history. They undergo difficult physical training. The training takes eight and a half weeks. It happens at Lackland Air Force Base. This base is in San Antonio, Texas.

Training at a tech school is required after basic training. The Air Force tech school is at Keesler Air Force Base in Biloxi, Mississippi. This training lasts sixty-six days. Students learn the basics of computer technology. They also learn about cybersecurity.

People become cyber specialists after completing this training. They report to an Air Force base and begin working. They can work toward certification in the field. Certification can give them more job opportunities. Later they can manage other specialists' work.

LOOKING AHEAD

Reserve careers have more flexible schedules than active-duty careers. This makes these careers attractive to many people. Sergeant Harlin Foster is a Cyber

Cyber specialists regularly repair and upgrade computer networks.

Systems Operations specialist. He works

on Nellis Air Force Base. This base is in

Las Vegas Valley, Nevada. Foster served

in the military before becoming a cyber

specialist. He enjoys the work-life balance

he has in this job. He has another job

outside of the Air Force. Sergeant Matthew Turner is also a cyber specialist. He works on Nellis Air Force Base too. He also sees the job's flexibility as a benefit. He says, "I was able to go to school and fulfill my reserve commitment."

Protecting military computer networks is an important job. Cybercriminals develop new ways to attack networks. Cyber specialists must keep up as technology evolves. The Air Force relies on these specialists. They will always be needed.

FIND OUT MORE

Forever Wingman

website: www.foreverwingman.com/3d0x2

This website offers details about Air Force Cyber Systems Operations jobs. The site features interviews with people in the field.

Today's Military

website: www.todaysmilitary.com/working/careers/cyber-operations-specialists

Cyber Systems Operations specialists are needed in all branches of the military. Learn more at this website.

The US Air Force

website: www.todaysmilitary.com/careers-benefits/career-fields/cybersecurity-and-information-technology

The US Air Force website provides information about a career in Cyber Systems Operations. It shares details about the education and training involved.

INTERVIEW WITH NAVY SAILORS

The US Navy has a blog called American Connections Media Outreach. The blog features interviews with sailors in the US Navy. The sailors talk about what they enjoy most about their jobs.

SENIOR CHIEF PETTY OFFICER JACOB ADAMS IS AN ELECTRONICS TECHNICIAN. HE OPERATES AND MAINTAINS NAVIGATIONAL EQUIPMENT ONBOARD A SUBMARINE. HE SAID:

"I enjoy teaching junior sailors how to . . . solve problems. There is a lot of camaraderie between the crew. It's a tight-knit community, and we become like family. Serving in the Navy means contributing to the defense of the nation and protecting interests worldwide. It's a job but also a way of life."

WILL WILEY IS A COMMANDING OFFICER. HE COMMANDS THE USS *JOHN WARNER* SUBMARINE. HE SAID:

"Being the commanding officer of one of our nation's submarines is the honor of a lifetime. I come to work every day with a smile on my face because of the outstanding men and women I have the opportunity to serve with . . . who all volunteered to keep our country safe."

JANE ABASOLA IS A SEAMAN. SHE MAINTAINS EQUIPMENT ON A NAVY SHIP. SHE SAID:

"I love doing my job every day and doing my best at it. I enjoy helping my fellow sailors. Serving in the Navy is being a part of a small [percentage] of people working together to protect the country. We are sacrificing a lot to be able to do this. The Navy takes care of you."

PETTY OFFICER 3RD CLASS LANE MORGAN IS A SONAR TECHNICIAN. SONAR IS THE USE OF SOUND WAVES TO MAP OBJECTS UNDERWATER. MORGAN OPERATES AND REPAIRS SUBMARINE SONAR EQUIPMENT. HE SAID:

"What I like most about working on a sub is [the] people I meet and interact with. . . . Serving in the Navy means being a part of something bigger than myself. Many of my family members served in the Air Force. I feel like as they are protecting [us] from the sky, I'm doing the same underwater. By my willingness to serve, I feel like I'm keeping others safe."

OTHER JOBS IN THE MILITARY

- Aircraft mechanic

- Air crew member

- Air traffic controller

- Armor assault vehicle officer

- Combat controller

- Cook

- Cyber operations officer

- Doctor

- Emergency medical technician

- Intelligence specialist

- Law enforcement

- Mobile heavy equipment mechanic

- Ship engineer

- Submarine readiness officer

Editor's Note: The US Department of Labor's Bureau of Labor Statistics provides information about hundreds of career options. The agency's Occupational Outlook Handbook describes the education and skill requirements, pay, and future outlook for each job. The Occupational Outlook Handbook can be found online at www.bls.gov/ooh.

GLOSSARY

artillery
large guns, such as cannons and mortars

buoy
a floating signal that helps steer boats

deploy
to send away from a home base, often overseas

enlisted
enrolled in the military

GPS
short for Global Positioning System, GPS is a navigational system that uses satellites

infantry
soldiers trained to fight on foot

mortar
a cannon with a short barrel

radar
a device that sends out radio waves to find objects, such as ships

surveillance
the act of watching someone or something carefully

terrorist
someone who uses violence to intimidate or threaten people

torpedo
a weapon that travels underwater to find its target

INDEX

IMAGE CREDITS

Cover: Sgt. Kandi Huggins/US Army

4–5: © Red Line Editorial

7: Patrick Albright/Maneuver Center of Excellence/Fort Benning Public Affairs/ US Army

8: Airman 1st Class Valerie Seelye/US Air Force

11: Spc. Jeremiah Woods/US Army

14: Lance Cpl. Dalton S. Swanbeck/ US Marine Corps/Defense Visual Information Distribution Service

17: Cpl. Shannon Kroening/US Marine Corps

18: Lance Cpl. Larisa Chavez/ US Marine Corps/Defense Visual Information Distribution Service

21: Sgt. Vanessa Austin/US Marine Corps/Defense Visual Information Distribution Service

22: Cpl. Adam Dublinske/Defense Visual Information Distribution Service

28: Scott T. Sturkol/Fort McCoy Public Affairs Office/US Army/Defense Visual Information Distribution Service

31: Spc. Lucas T. Swihart/US Army

32: © Joseph Sohm/ Shutterstock Images

35: © W. Scott McGill/ Shutterstock Images

36: Staff Sgt. Nelia Chappell/US Army

40: Mass Communication Specialist Seaman Aiyana S. Paschal/US Navy/ US Department of Defense

43: Mass Communication Specialist 2nd Class James R. Evans/US Navy

44: Chief Mass Communication Specialist Sam Shavers/US Navy

47: Chief Mass Communication Specialist Keith W. DeVinney/US Navy

48: Mass Communication Specialist 1st Class Rachel McMarr/US Navy

52: Petty Officer 1st Class Matthew S. Masaschi/US Coast Guard

55: Chief Petty Officer David Mosley/ US Coast Guard

56: © aviahuisman/ Shutterstock Images

59: Petty Officer 2nd Class Patrick Kelley/US Coast Guard/Defense Visual Information Distribution Service

60: Petty Officer 1st Class Fred Sullivan/US Coast Guard

65: Senior Airman Cody Martin/US Air National Guard/Defense Visual Information Service

67: Tech. Sgt. Matthew Plew/US Air Force

68: Airman 1st Class Krystal Ardrey/US Air Force

71: Staff Sgt. Lealan Buehrer/U.S. Air National Guard/Defense Visual Information Distribution Service

ABOUT THE AUTHOR

Roberta Baxter has written more than forty-five books about science and history for students of all ages. She knows and admires people who work in the military. She lives in Colorado Springs, Colorado, which has five military bases.